WORKING *with* SMEs

WORKING
with SMEs

*A Guide to Gathering and Organizing Content
from Subject Matter Experts*

SECOND EDITION

Peggy Salvatore

BALBOA.
PRESS
A DIVISION OF HAY HOUSE

Balboa Press books may be ordered through booksellers or by contacting:

Balboa Press
A Division of Hay House
1663 Liberty Drive
Bloomington, IN 47403
www.balboapress.com
1 (877) 407-4847

Because of the dynamic nature of the Internet, any web addresses or links contained in this book may have changed since publication and may no longer be valid. The views expressed in this work are solely those of the author and do not necessarily reflect the views of the publisher, and the publisher hereby disclaims any responsibility for them.

The author of this book does not dispense medical advice or prescribe the use of any technique as a form of treatment for physical, emotional, or medical problems without the advice of a physician, either directly or indirectly. The intent of the author is only to offer information of a general nature to help you in your quest for emotional and spiritual well-being. In the event you use any of the information in this book for yourself, which is your constitutional right, the author and the publisher assume no responsibility for your actions.

Certain stock imagery © Thinkstock.
Any people depicted in stock imagery provided by Thinkstock are models, and such images are being used for illustrative purposes only.

Printed in the United States of America.

ISBN: 978-1-5043-2671-1 (sc)
ISBN: 978-1-5043-2673-5 (hc)
ISBN: 978-1-5043-2672-8 (e)

Library of Congress Control Number: 2015900749

Balboa Press rev. date: 01/20/2015

DEDICATION

This book is dedicated to my children,
Ben, Ellie and Molly.

CONTENTS

ACKNOWLEDGMENTS

I owe a tremendous amount to many people, especially all the subject matter experts with whom I've had the pleasure of working. I've learned training by working with some very gifted instructional designers, trainers and facilitators, truly experiencing "earn while you learn" with some of the best in the industry. It's been an exciting journey.

First, and most importantly, is a wonderful friend and mentor, Jonena Relth, who served as a leadership evangelist and President of TBD Consulting, Inc. from 1991 until her retirement in 2014. Jonena signed on as co-author for the first edition of this book. While she still occasionally can be found online chatting about leadership and training issues, she is mostly a lady of leisure now enjoying her time in beautiful Southern California. No acknowledgment of others can begin without recognizing her influence on contributing advice and content, especially to Chapter 7 where many of TBD's tools and charts have provided the basis for what exists there today.

Beyond Jonena, I owe a special note of gratitude to several people for encouraging me and, in some cases, pushing me to get this second edition ready for prime time. Their order of appearance in no way reflects the importance of their contributions.

Much gratitude is due my primary editor and dear friend, Robin Warshaw. Robin is a truly gifted writer and editor; she is, in fact, a writer's editor because she leaves your voice intact, scrubs the glaring grammatical errors and inconsistencies, and questions the value and context of content. She's a pro. Thank you, Robin!

Some of the changes in this edition are the work of the quality control maven at TBD, Heather Rodriguez. Heather's impeccable line editing made its way into this edition, and I am grateful for her contribution.

Special thanks are due to Michael Kolowich of KnowledgeVision who promoted the book and topic early in this effort, and encouraged people to take a serious look at the effect this issue has on knowledge transfer and institutional knowledge management. Thank you so much, Michael!

Although last here, Nathan Eckel, past president of ASTD's Philadelphia chapter, actually appears first chronologically in the list of people who encouraged this book. He provided insight and guidance early in the concept phase. This book was partially inspired by one of his own, *Open Source Instructional Design*. Nathan is in the business of teaching SMEs how to do instructional design and when I was looking for information on how to work with SMEs, I turned to his book.

INTRODUCTION

Working with SMEs is intended as a guide and tool for instructional designers (IDs) who write corporate training programs, subject matter experts (SMEs), and the people who manage them. As such, it is designed so that training practitioners can pick it up and use it easily. Some training designers might be tempted to go straight to Chapter 7 and just pull out the tools; you can do that. However, the rhyme and reason of *Working with SMEs* is in the rest of the book and understanding the hows and whys behind the tools will help you use them well.

Why not several books addressing different audiences? Quite simply, the content is interwoven, and there are perspectives and tools in all parts that training designers, SMEs and managers will find helpful. I strived to create one handy reference that training departments and training consulting firms will be able to hand out to people in their organizations who have been tasked with writing training for their company. I believe that having all the pieces for *Working with SMEs* in one place will help each party better understand the other, something essential to a seamless process.

In addition to providing tips and tools, this book strives to promote understanding between training designers and SMEs in these two complementary but different roles – two roles that, if not well understood by both parties, can lead to a longer, more expensive and ultimately less effective training product. When training designers and SMEs work together with a common understanding of their roles, not only do the two parties benefit, the process is more enjoyable, and the learner will come away with more of what they really need – all that valuable information tucked away in the SME's brain.

CHAPTER 1.

The Rationale: Journalism as an ID Training Ground

Subject matter experts are some of my favorite people. That is why this book is a labor of love. A geek at heart, I am fascinated by someone who hasn't looked up from a petri dish in 40 years, or someone who has been tinkering in the guts of the financial system, awash in banking acronyms. Admittedly, my eyes are glazed over for the first few weeks of our relationship while the expert waxes eloquently about their passion, but I am fascinated nonetheless.

I started my career as a journalist; in retrospect, it is an excellent training ground for instructional designers (IDs). Journalism prepares you to go into new situations, learn new things and ask basic questions to understand how something works – all so you can explain it to others. Like journalists, instructional designers may eventually acquire a level of expertise themselves.

And, like journalism, corporate and organizational training is about telling people things that other people know and do. Instructional design is *how* you tell it. *Working with SMEs* is learning *what* to tell. A great training program masters both of these pieces. The training field has a few standard models about how to structure training; there is precious little on how to gather content in a systematic way.

The science of technical documentation is a field in itself. When you are *Working with SMEs*, the tools for capturing and organizing information are essential. Many training departments and consulting firms have processes and templates to standardize technical documentation. Chapter 7 of this book is based on some of those tools and techniques. However, the whole technique of working with subject matter experts is more intricate than simple technical documentation, and therefore needs its *own* methodology.

Models for designing training are just that – models that reflect a perfect structure and methodology for imparting knowledge, skills and attitudes. Most instructional designers create training programs using the ADDIE model – Analyze, Design, Develop, Implement and Evaluate, or some variation of it. Therefore, the model for *Working with SMEs* is built on the ADDIE structure to determine what good information gathering looks like.

Working with SMEs and the ADDIE Methodology

A training program has two parts:

1. Instructional design is how to *structure and relate* knowledge, skills and attitudes (KSAs) in a systematic way.

2. *Working with SMEs* is about how to *collect* information from the *right* people, *select* what is relevant and *organize it* in a systematic way.

As part of the information collection process, training departments usually develop templates for review cycles and signoffs with subject matter experts, but there is not an established methodology in ID literature about how to select the SME, then collect and organize information.

Instructional designers have their favorite models for designing training, and they are usually some variation of the ADDIE model. The *Working with SMEs* methodology covers the entire ADDIE spectrum. The intense information-gathering phase begins at Analysis, in which you collect most information from subject matter experts. Content gathering carries through the process as you organize content and refine your program through development to evaluation, including review and sign-off milestones.

Specifically, in the Analysis phase, you list resources, including the people who will serve as your subject matter experts. During this preliminary phase, the information you gather influences the project scope based on what you are learning. At this point, subject matter experts provide you with data, notes and information that you may be supplementing with focus groups, surveys and other data collection tools.

By the time you reach the Design phase, the specifications are driven by your audience, learning objectives and the activities that are best suited to achieve your overall performance goals[1]. During this phase, clients[2] approve graphics, software and any other criteria for presentation of the program, and SMEs are in the review cycle.

After Development, both the SMEs and the project stakeholders should sign off on all phases of the project before implementation. Ideally, the formal Evaluation phase occurs at least 30 to 60 days after Implementation to find out if learning "stuck." Based on the results of the Evaluation, the program may require content adjustments which frequently involve a second iteration of the ADDIE process.

---

[1] We use the term *performance goals* for the high-level behavioral objectives of the training program; some Training designers may use other terms such as *terminal objectives.*

[2] The term client refers to the entity that is paying for the training program. If you are a training company, the client is an external customer; if you are a training department in a large organization, the client is an internal customer or department.

Chart 1.1: Where the *Working with SMEs* Methodology Fits in the ADDIE Model

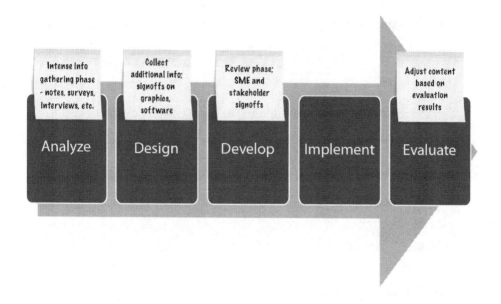

What Should a *Working with SMEs* Methodology Include?

To develop the model for *Working with SMEs*, first I needed to establish what good information gathering looks like. A best-practices model should contain these four elements that are common to all content-gathering efforts for a training program.

A *Working with SMEs* methodology:

- Provides instructional designers and subject matter experts with a framework for collecting and reviewing content

- Describes the qualities of a good SME and how to work with them

- Works within the existing ID system (we are using ADDIE) and takes into account the already-existing body of knowledge and commonly accepted best practices

Includes a framework for managing the content collection and review cycle

Taking those requirements into consideration, this book is structured around meeting these goals. Let's begin our journey in developing a methodology for *Working with SMEs* by first defining The Perfect SME.

CHAPTER 2.

The Perfect SME

The Perfect SME has three essential qualities. The Perfect SME is:

- The most knowledgeable and articulate person about that topic in the organization

- One who has, or will be given, the time to work with you

- Willing and possibly looking forward to being part of the training design process

If your SME is missing any of these three ingredients, you may have trouble. If that happens and you don't have an alternate SME, we offer tips and tools throughout this book to help you negotiate those issues effectively.

First, whether you've been dealt the Perfect SME or not, you'll need to establish deadlines and clear lines of communication for fact-checking and sign-offs at the very beginning of your relationship. It is unlikely the SME will be tracking those things, and you may not have other supports in place to do it for you. Your project scope or Project Charter should include details about deadlines and lines of responsibility that can help define the relationship.[3]

As the instructional designer on the project, you will find yourself managing up, managing laterally and possibly managing outside your department to make things happen. Setting expectations and deadlines up front will make the process smoother and less harrowing for you.

Which brings us back to the trouble with SMEs...yes, even the perfect ones who meet all three of the essential qualities.

The Trouble with SMEs

The trouble with SMEs starts when experts look up from the petri dish or financial spreadsheet and try to tell you what they are doing. So while they are rattling on about *HARP* and *bundling* and *translational research*, you are looking at them and thinking, "Huh?" They have reached a level of expertise in which they are Unconscious Competents – that is, they are so well-informed on their subjects they don't even realize how much they know. It is likely that the SME you are working with has forgotten more

---

[3] A sample project charter can be found in Chapter 7.

than you will ever know about the content of the program you are writing.

This is a gift and a curse. Here's why.

The Four Stages of Learning Model and Your SME

In case you aren't familiar with the levels of competence[4], here are the types of SME competence you may encounter:

1. Unconscious Incompetent – doesn't know what she doesn't know

2. Conscious Incompetent – knows what she doesn't know

3. Conscious Competent – knows what she knows

4. Unconscious Competent – doesn't know what she knows

---

[4] The four levels of competence are known in training literature as The Four Stages of Learning. Noel Burch of Gordon Training International is credited with developing this model in the 1970s. Others, such as Abraham Maslow, have also been credited with developing it.

Chart 2.1: The Four Stages of Learning Model

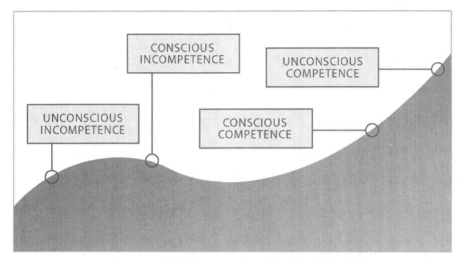

Credit: http://seesparkbox.com/uploads/article_uploads/responsive-dip-graph-1b.jpg

According to The Four Stages of Learning model (Chart 2.1), the Unconscious Competent is the highest level on an ascending trajectory of knowledge. For that reason, these very smart people are usually assigned the job of acting as your SME. However, when you look at these four stages of learning on a chart that tracks both *knowledge* and *awareness* (Chart 2.2), you can see where your SME might fall short of your ideal for the purposes of gathering information in a systematic way.

Chart 2.2: The Ideal SME Model

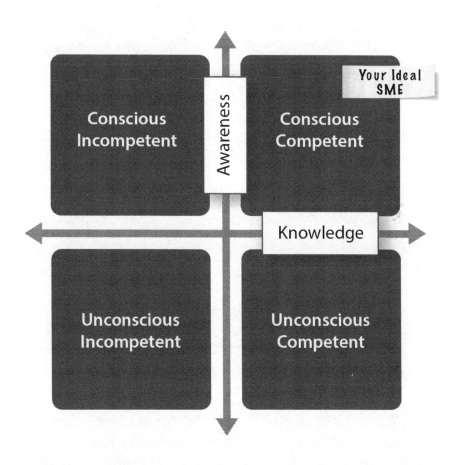

Where is Your SME on the Continuum of Knowledge?

Ideally, your SME is on the third level of the four stages of learning continuum and is a Conscious Competent. That means she is aware of what she knows, and she is able to tell you. Since such a SME is still on the learning curve herself, not having reached the state where her knowledge is unconscious, she is closer to her own training and remembers what it is like to be a naïve learner. By remembering what it is like to not know, the SME will better remember how she acquired the knowledge or skill that is the subject of your training program, and by extension, how to explain it in a linear way to you.

Briefly, here is how a SME at each level of competence will affect your information gathering process:

Unconscious Competent: When you are gifted with a SME who has risen to career heights in a specialized field and can still explain what she knows, you have truly unearthed a gem. You will both find the tools in this book helpful to organize that a lifetime of knowledge into small, digestible, relevant chunks for you and your learners. Simply, she is such a vast repository of information that she really does not know how much she knows and how well she knows it. It is your job to unearth the gems and help her break it down into simple steps.

Conscious Competent: When you have been given the bright, up-and-coming SME who is still ascending the ladder of knowledge, these tools will help you focus on the important pieces of information that you need to assemble for your learners and identify the additional resources to fill in gaps as they arise.

Conscious Incompetent: When you are faced with a SME who lacks the needed knowledge, we have some tips in the next chapter for that situation. Our recommendation, though, is that you search to find a Conscious Competent SME. It will save you time and effort in the short and long run.

Unconscious Incompetent: It happens. You can be given a know-nothing SME. This is the worst of all possible worlds. We'll discuss how to deal with this situation in the next chapter, too.

CHAPTER 3.

Working with the Four Stages of Competence

When you begin writing a training program, in almost every case you will be assigned a 3rd or 4th level SME – a Conscious or Unconscious Competent. Most of our discussion in this chapter is dedicated to that assumption.

For just a minute or two, though, let's contemplate the remote possibility that you get a 1st or 2nd level competent as your SME, the Incompetent. This won't take long because your relationship will be short.

The 1st Level SME – The Unconscious Incompetent

Think about this for a moment: you've been assigned a SME for your training program who is unaware of what he doesn't know. This SME isn't really a SME at all, but whoever assigned him thinks he is. He doesn't know much of anything about your topic. While it won't take you long to figure out he doesn't know jack about your subject, it might take you a little longer to disentangle yourself and get someone who knows Jack, or even his sister Jill.

Telltale Signs of the Unconscious Incompetent

- You ask for information and you get nothing.

- You ask for information and the SME talks about something unrelated.

- You can't focus the SME on the topic because he doesn't know anything about the issue at hand.

How to Deal with an Unconscious Incompetent

1. **Ask for a replacement SME.** Speak privately with your customer and tell him you need a different SME. Working with this person is wasting both your time and the company's money.

2. **Provide documented proof.** If you're not successful with fix #1, have a backup plan: Show documented evidence demonstrating why the SME is not the right person for the project. Be sure to include specific instances that show his lack of relevant knowledge, lack of responsiveness or inept and irrelevant answers to your requests.

3. **Restate the information you need** and the qualities of the person who is likely to have it. Something may be awry if this wasn't done up front. So, make the best of this opportunity to reboot and help your customer understand what you need to develop the training they require. If necessary or possible, interview a few potential replacements before moving forward. It is possible the people responsible for assigning a SME may not understand enough about the subject to know if they are choosing the right person.

4. **Tread very cautiously** if the Unconscious Incompetent is a leader and/or well-liked. This situation could be very sensitive. You may want to state officially that you need another SME. Put on your most politically-astute hat and use a creative, face-saving excuse to allow the SME to be removed or bow out gracefully.

The 2nd Level SME – The Conscious Incompetent

A 2nd level SME is much preferable to a 1st level SME simply because his lack of knowledge is on the table. You may be assigned a SME who is not appropriate for the subject at hand and you both know it. That is very good news, because together you can usually find the right person.

Telltale Signs of the Conscious Incompetent

- The first and most obvious sign is that as soon as you approach him for expertise on your topic, he tells you he is not the right person to be talking to you.

- He tries to fulfill the assignment because he has been asked by a manager, and so he looks for answers and information for what you need. Neither of you are sure the information is correct, and it is time-consuming.

- He knows he lacks the expertise you need, but he tries to hide it from you and the person who selected him. This is the worst possible scenario with a 2nd level Conscious Incompetent, because you will initially be fed bad information and eventually realize it – hopefully sooner rather than later.

How to Deal With a Conscious Incompetent

1. If the SME tells you he isn't the right person, you have an ally to find an appropriate expert.[4]

2. In the second case, when your SME tries to fill the assignment out of a sense of responsibility, encourage him to enlist others to help. Then you will probably be able to migrate your project to working with a genuine expert after a few frustrating review sessions of work prepared with input from the Conscious Incompetent. We call these "aarrrgghhh" sessions. Both of you will be frustrated until

you are given someone more knowledgeable. Depending on the organization's structure and the authority of your SME, the two of you may be able to solve this problem on your own. If not, together compile a request for another SME that contains enough detail to enlist a more appropriate person.

3. When the SME is trying to hide his lack of knowledge, you have a problem. He is probably trying to save face and may even be afraid his job is in jeopardy. He may have good reason to hide his incompetence from you. You will need to approach your customer with a list of things you need to know. Show that your SME doesn't have answers that work or make sense, and ask the customers to collaborate with you to find the right person. Since it is likely neither your customer nor the SME's manager has the time to help you find the information you need, you must act efficiently in becoming allies with your customers to search for a new expert. Unfortunately, this process will take time and affect your project timeline.

Advantages and Disadvantages of Working with 1st and 2nd Level Incompetents

The advantages of working with an incompetent SME, no matter the reason, is that if you explain the SME's lack of knowledge and experience clearly to your managers and his, you are likely to find an appropriate expert. When you work with people to find answers, you will be valued as an instructional designer who can directly handle problems and solve them in order to write a substantial, valid program.

The disadvantages of working with an incompetent SME are listed above and briefly can be summed up as frustrating, time-wasting experiences that net no real value to move you toward the objective of writing your training program. Accept that it can happen, know that you usually can identify the problem quickly, and that you can also usually solve it.

The 3rd Level SME: The Conscious Competent

The 3rd level competent is truly the instructional designer's best friend. The Conscious Competent knows what you need to include in your program. He understands how to explain it to you. And he will tell you what you need to know in a logical sequence. This allows you the luxury of doing what you do so well – designing a program that best communicates the material to the learners. Consider yourself lucky.

Telltale Signs of the Conscious Competent

- He knows he has been assigned to provide you with information to build a training program and he has assembled what you need.

- He can explain anything that isn't obvious from the well-organized materials he has given you.

- He can review the draft curriculum you have created from his materials, find the holes and help you fill them in one pass.

How to Deal with a Conscious Competent

1. Read the materials the SME gives you and be prepared to ask questions. Be forthright about material that is difficult for you to understand. Ask follow-up questions to gain clarification.

2. Be organized with an instructionally-sound specification document for your design so his information merely needs to be inserted.

3. Be ready and willing to adjust your design based on additional information as it arises.

4. Be specific and brief with your questions, prompt in your meetings, and stick to the review schedule. Help keep the SME on track and make review materials easy to use and correct.

5. Thank the SME. Be courteous.

The 4th Level SME: The Unconscious Competent

This SME is commonly the person you will be working with. The Unconscious Competent SME has a lot of advantages. Most of all, he knows everything you need for your program…and more.

But this particular SME presents challenges as well. It is those challenges that drive most of this book's content. When you are dealing with an Unconscious Competent SME, you need to be very organized, do your homework, and dig into the topic so you ask the right questions to get the information your learners need.

Telltale Signs of the Unconscious Competent

- He talks quickly, throwing around a lot of terms and concepts that are unfamiliar to you. He doesn't seem to realize, or care, that you are a layperson.

- He can be impatient or annoyed if you can't keep up.

- The material he gives you to use for your program is high level and not in language that is appropriate for your learners.

- You have to do a lot of basic research to figure out what he is talking about.

How to Deal with an Unconscious Competent

This advice is best practice for collecting and organizing content and will be supported with tips and tools in subsequent chapters.

1. When you don't understand a term or concept, stop the SME and ask him to explain. Make an audio recording and transcription of all meetings and interviews, if allowed. Take good notes, even when recording.

2. Ask for written materials and resources so you can do research and learn the basics on your own.

3. Create a glossary and a list of acronyms for yourself; add it to the training program for your learners. In the case of written materials, the glossary can appear as call-out boxes in the text. In the case of eLearning programs or electronic documents, terminology can appear as rollovers and pop-ups throughout the program.

4. If you are unsure about your content, ask the SME to review it at frequent intervals. That way, you won't travel down the wrong path for any length of time.

5. Take good notes, reference uncommon knowledge using footnotes or endnotes, and stick to a schedule.

6. Keep a sense of humor and a positive attitude.

7. Be thorough and keep calm.

Advantages and Disadvantages of Working with 3rd and 4th Level Competents

	Advantages	Disadvantages
Conscious Competent 3rd Level Competent	• They will have patience with your level of ignorance. • They can point you to basic materials to help you up the learning curve. • They understand the learning process behind how to learn the subject.	• You may still have to go to someone else to find out some of the answers you need to build a comprehensive and rich training program. • They may not understand the bigger picture (yet) about how what they do solves organizational or professional problems in their field. You may not be able to take your training program to the next level and start to move your learners toward being part of the solution in your subject matter area.

| Unconscious Competent 4th Level Competent | • They know more than anybody else in the organization about your subject.

• They know where the problems lie and usually how to fix them.

• You can build a very rich training program that helps learners solve problems.

• They tend to be big-picture thinkers and have a global view of what you are doing. | • They know things you need to know, and they inadvertently may not be telling you. You need to ask enough questions to uncover it.

• They frequently don't have the time you need to explain the basics because they are invaluable to the organization. You'll need to do some research after talking to them.

• Occasionally they don't have the patience to explain what they know, which is usually why they are in organizations doing things and not in academic institutions explaining it to students. |

SMEs Are People Too

Even on our best days, we aren't always at our best. That is true for your subject matter expert, too. Whether it is part of their personality or a momentary temperamental aberration, sometimes your SME will not be wholly cooperative or informative. This is true for SMEs across the entire spectrum of competence.

You may have a highly conscious competent who is not communicating well or a conscious incompetent who is frustrated and doing their best. No matter the circumstances, like any of our relationships, it is helpful to have a few tools in the interpersonal toolbox to deal with temperaments and situations.

Here is a table of some common pitfalls and the strategies to help overcome them.

SME	Pitfall	Strategy
Speedy SME	The SME becomes impatient with you controlling the pace of the session.	• Explain that less skilled personnel will complete the training process. You need to capture all of the details to make that possible. • Reassure the SME that documentation will take less time if you move slowly and steadily so you can capture all the information the first time. • Use humor, when appropriate, to help diffuse frustration.
Scattered SME	The SME does not think sequentially and sees the process as so complex and variable that it cannot possibly be captured in steps.	• Reassure the SME that it is your job to make sense out of a complex process and you have experience doing that. • Guide the info-gathering session using a process map.*see Chapter 7 • Encourage the SME to show you the steps so you can get a feel for the process.
Shortcut SME	The SME has been doing this so long that she uses shortcuts a novice could never follow and might not be best practice for the organization.	• Re-focus the SME by explaining that you are to document only best practices for the company that can be followed by the audience who will definitely include people not as experienced as the SME. • Request the SME demonstrate the best practice process.

Defensive SME	The SME feels their job is threatened. If they tell you anything, they run the risk of losing their job.	• Reinforce the value of the SME's expertise. • Use a non-threatening scenario like, "Imagine that starting next week I am going to be your personal assistant, and you want me to do this task for you."
Not Quite the Expert SME	The SME does not really know the best practice or does not think they know the best practice.	• Discuss the situation with the Supervisor. Identify an alternate SME who may know the process better. • For some new processes, the best practice may not yet be well established. Reassure the SME that they are the most qualified person. • Review the resulting information with other experienced personnel including supervisors as either an interim review or part of the final review process.
Overcommitted SME	The SME consistently misses or is late for appointments or is overloaded with regular work responsibilities and is grouchy about making time for the documentation session.	• Do your best to empathize with the SME's situation and assure him you will not waste his time. • Make sure the SME knows what you will be doing in the Info-gathering session so he can have documents ready. • Call and/or email the day before to confirm and remind the SME of the appointment.

		• If the issue persists, review the situation with the supervisor. Often, the SME is trying to juggle conflicting priorities. The supervisor can intervene. • Always thank the SME for their time and commitment.
SME Interrupted	The SME is constantly being interrupted during the info-gathering session.	• Reassure the SME that documentation will take less time if both of you are focused. • Conduct the session away from the workstation (if documenting software, make sure the system functions the same in the alternate location). • If you cannot move, ask the SME to forward his phone and tack a do not disturb sign on his cubicle or office door. • Let the SME select the meeting time. Be flexible and work at a time when interruptions are less likely. This may be very early or late in the day. • Limit the sessions to 2 or 3 hours, at most, so it does not interfere with an entire work day and the SME can give you one-on-one, quality time.
Reckless Reviewer	When presented with a draft of the training program, the SME just visually scans it rather than validating that it is correct.	• Set the expectations of a thorough review up front. • Spend time with the SME to review the drafted data in your info-gathering session. Read each step and have the SME perform it, if applicable.

CHAPTER 4.

The Instructional Designer as Subject Matter Expert

If you are the smartest person in the room, you are in the wrong room.

Instructional designers are subject matter experts. As an instructional designer, your subject matter expertise is in the training and performance field. You are the expert in collecting, organizing and designing learning experiences to communicate information to learners. But, in actuality, to the rest of the world – all the software engineers, financiers, scientists, top sales performers, nurses and architects of the world - you are a generalist.

A generalist is someone who knows a little bit about a lot of things. As an instructional designer, you need to know enough about how things work to be able to figure out how something else works and explain it to others. And if you don't know how things work, you need to be curious enough to want to find out.

Great instructional designers don't just care about their learners; they care about their subject matter and treat it with the respect it deserves. Instructional designers are charged with handling critical information and passing it on to others who need to know it, too. It's like being the United States Postal Service – you are transferring something very valuable, and you want it to arrive intact. Think of your careful information gathering process and well-designed training program as bubble wrap.

Instructional Designers Have Levels of Competence, Too

Instructional designers are on the learning curve, too. You may be a Conscious or Unconscious Competent. (We are assuming that since you are reading a book in your field that you are not incompetent – conscious or otherwise!)

Due to the nature of what you do, which is transferring learning, you most likely know what you know, how you learned it and can tell others. With training designers who have a few years of experience, you are especially close to your education. You are at the stage where you follow the ADDIE model closely and write down all the steps of your training programs expressly. The practice of working through the ADDIE phases as an exercise and a guideline for your training program is a very good one, and it will help you as you collect and organize content while *Working with SMEs*.

For those who have been writing training for many years, you may automatically jump right in and start writing a training program – even designing it in your head - while not specifically and overtly outlining some of the design phases. This practice may work for those who are intimately familiar with their material, but it has some of the same pitfalls as those you experience with your 4th level unconscious competent SME. A 4th level ID competent may inadvertently miss some of the basic steps by assuming your colleagues already understand those steps. Be aware of this pitfall and make sure to stick close to best practices by purposely creating a design document applying ADDIE – or whatever design model your company uses – to all your training programs. That way you are sharing your thinking process with everyone on the project so they can follow your design faithfully and have input, too.

Differences Between the 3rd and 4th Level ID

It is important to know whether you are a 3rd or 4th level ID, and whether those around you are 3rd or 4th level IDs. It will impact understanding how you develop training and how they may develop training so that you can avoid missing steps.

The tools and tips for *Working with SMEs* are applied consciously to an ADDIE model. By adhering to a best practices model, you can avoid pitfalls and bridge any knowledge gaps between 3rd and 4th level training designers to keep your training program development running smoothly.

The main differences between the 3rd and 4th level instructional design SMEs is that 3rd level competents will tend to spend more time in the planning design phase of the project, while 4th level instructional design SMEs are more likely to jump right in and start development. The main reason for this difference is that, after years of creating training, some of the planning is automatically worked out in the head of a 4th level ID. Just like the trouble with Unconscious Competent subject matter experts, when the 4th level instructional design SME does not explicitly write out the design plan, those working with her will have trouble following her logic and providing either the content or the managerial guidance that contributes to a productive team environment.

The 3rd Level Instructional Designer

A 3rd level ID brings a lot of the same attributes to the table as the 3rd level SME – they know what they know and can be explicit in developing training according to best practices.

A 3rd level ID will studiously make an assessment of the training needs, develop performance goals in cooperation with the client, and work with the SME to develop content that helps learners reach expressed learning objectives.

The *Working with SMEs* methodology will be very easy to apply for the 3rd level ID, as it follows the analysis, design, development, implement and evaluate phases logically. For those who use an abbreviated design and development process, such as the Successive Approximation Model (SAM), the tools are applicable to their data collection and organization efforts.

The 4ᵗʰ Level Expert Instructional Designer

An expert ID may be the person in charge of designing the training programs in your organization. You are the training program's architect. You are the one tasked with the following:

- Aligning training programs to corporate goals

- Understanding the impact of learning on meeting those goals

- Understanding what good performance should look like

- Assuming ultimate responsibility for reaching corporate targets against preset measures

The expert ID is a strategist. When she brings her knowledge to bear on your efforts to design training, the ID is the training architect for the organization who is thinking about the big picture. She is concerned about getting to performance goals and meeting those targets with your program. And sometimes, after spending a lot of time in the world of theory, the expert ID may become an unconscious competent.

> **Tip:** When the program architect is an unconscious competent, you may find it helpful to unpack their knowledge using some of the same tools that you use with your SMEs to get what you need from them to meet their goals for the program you are designing.

The Trouble with IDs

My favorite expression that relates across all business roles and relationships is: *If you are the smartest person in the room, you are in the wrong room.* For an ID who stuck around to read this section, that should be your mantra. As a SME who is reading this section, this should be flattering to you, if you are susceptible to such things (which many true SMEs are not!).

In any event, training designers do not want to be the smartest person in the room but aspire to find rooms with very smart people in them. They are smart enough to appreciate their SME and understand them. That's the job of the ID – to understand the subject matter well enough to ask questions in an organized way. Done well, the ID will get a brain dump from the SME that can be captured.

Training designers don't need to know everything, just the things that pertain to the training program. But, given your naiveté in a field, you are likely to ask a lot of peripheral questions to try to understand context. Or you may go down some paths that lead nowhere because you don't exactly understand the relevance of detailed information to the big picture. When you think you are going down a rabbit hole, say so.

Hiring a Dedicated SME

A dedicated SME is someone hired by a training firm so it has full-time access to topic expertise within the training firm's own organization. As the term implies, this SME is dedicated to helping you build the training program.

This term is relevant mostly to freestanding independent training consulting firms whose core expertise is performance and organizational development, not the area of the training topic. If you are an internal training department in an engineering firm, for example, the expertise you need is already your firm's core competency. It is expected that your SMEs are available, so there is no need to hire one just to work with the training department.

However, if you are a full-time training and organizational development company working on a training program for an engineering firm, you may find yourself hiring an engineering consultant to provide you with the kind of expertise you need to deliver a top-quality training program.

How to use a dedicated SME:

1. Analyze phase: the dedicated SME is present to ask questions and direct the conversations.

2. Design phase: the dedicated SME helps organize the content and clarify the objectives.

3. During data collection, the dedicated SME checks the client's materials for accuracy, clarity and gaps.

4. Development phase: the dedicated SME does the first "content dump" by putting the material in your framework.

5. Development phase: the dedicated SME validates your activities and assessment tests.

6. The dedicated SME serves as the liaison with your assigned SMEs during the review process.

7. Implementation Phase: especially in the case of instructor-led training, the dedicated SME may also serve as a facilitator for the program due to her expertise.

8. Evaluation phase: the dedicated SME can assess the program's effectiveness.

Note that the presence of a dedicated SME does not alter any of the process steps for *Working with SMEs*, but it gives the instructional designer confidence when wading in unfamiliar or intimidating topic areas by having a subject matter expert assigned solely to assist her in writing her training program.

When to use a dedicated SME:

- When the training designers are not confident that they can understand a complex or intimidating topic using the regular steps for *Working with SMEs*.

- When your client SMEs may not be available for the amount of time you need to fully understand your topic due to the demands of their regular assignments.

- When your client SMEs may not have time for thorough reviews of your material.

- When your client SMEs are in disagreement and differences in material need to be negotiated.

Things to consider when hiring a dedicated SME:

- You are sure that the subject matter is incomprehensible to you without one.

- The project price supports it and the client is willing to pay for it.

- The SME works well with the client's SMEs.

- The SME supports the firm's training mission and fits into the culture.

- You are certain that there are not enough SMEs with enough time in the organization you are working with to help you gather and review the content.

A dedicated SME can be a valuable asset in helping you create a strong product when those conditions exist. As an added bonus, after you've hired a SME in a specific topic area, you have now strengthened your hand in that field and can attract other clients with similar needs. It is a move you may consider when you are building competency as a single-topic training design house.

The cost and dedication to this effort is substantial, but if you are working with a client who is willing to pay for you to acquire this competency by paying for the expertise, you can yield the benefits without incurring the cost.

CHAPTER 5.

For SMEs: How You Can Make the Process Smoother

For those who are intellectually curious and love to learn, Instructional Design is a dream job. Working with you as their SME is very interesting for them.

Now, let's switch gears and talk directly to you, the SMEs. Training designers are experts in collecting, organizing and relating information in a logical and comprehensible way, but they are not PhD neurobiologists. They get to play in your sandbox, and if you are lucky, they majored in microbiology as an undergrad in college. But when it comes to your area of expertise, they are not the smartest people in the room.

For someone who is intellectually curious and loves to learn, instructional design is a dream job. Working with you is very interesting for him. He is going to learn a lot from you so he can teach it to others. But the ID doesn't know your subject yet, and they may or may not have a good base of knowledge in your area of expertise to ask some foundational questions. If your ID needs some background, provide him with resources so he can study on his own time. It is not a wise use of either of your time for you to teach him the basics of chemistry, for example. It is in his job description to learn the basics on his own before diving in. Don't be afraid to give the ID homework; in fact, it is a good idea to do so.

The ID's Challenge

The challenge of the ID is to learn just enough to know what information to collect, how to organize it and how to create a learning environment that makes that information attainable by others. That is the expertise of the ID. He is a master learner and organizer. He is a student of human behavior and good communicator. You, as a SME, might be good at those things, too, but you may not be as good as the ID is at all of them. That is, after all, *his* job.

As a SME, you have been in your profession a long time and most likely you got to the top of your field by already practicing good communication and organizational skills. For the purpose of this book, we'll review some basic rules of business behavior in the context of your role as a SME for your organization's training program later on in this chapter under Tips for Working with Your Instructional Designer.

Does a SME Need to Be an Instructional Designer?

The short answer is no. In fact, the long answer is no.

It is the job of the ID to conceptualize and plan a well-orchestrated training program. It is your job to fill in the blanks. If you find that you are having trouble whittling down what you know to fill in the blanks, or you can't fill in the blanks as requested, the ID needs to come up with a better plan. A well-designed training program will make it fairly obvious to you exactly what steps the learner will be taking to learn the material. It will also be obvious what is being requested of you.

The ID should be able to make clear to you the following:

• Objectives and goals of the training program

• Information needed to achieve the learning

• Process and timetable for the project

The ID is depending on you for content in your area of expertise. Instructional design is an area of expertise all its own, and it is possible that your ID has a master's degree or PhD in Instructional Design. Learning theory is an area of expertise that is driving the training program's development, and you are not expected to know that. Your subject matter expertise is invaluable, and that is your role.

Side note: Since most of us have some computer literacy, you may be called on to work directly in an application such as a slide presentation application or create videos to help build the training program. Companies who are short-staffed or who may not understand the value of hiring a learning professional may ask you to build the learning. If so, be sure to ask for guidance from the professional training staff at your organization, if you have them. You may eventually acquire some degree of expertise in working in these programs, but that is not your role for our purposes here. There are also books on the topic of instructional design for SMEs which you may find valuable if you find that you are being tasked with some training development work.

What to Expect from Your ID

It is the ID's job to ask a lot of questions. He may be trying to get context and may ask a lot of questions to tie the learning to other things. In adult learning, it is good practice to give context to the learner by relating new knowledge to things they already know. However, if you find the ID's questions wander too far afield to be relevant to the training at hand, tell him so.

Conversely, and probably more commonly, the ID may not be asking enough questions. He may not know to ask you certain questions to help him gain context and background. If you are talking and he has a quizzical look, stop and ask if he needs clarification. The ID may be waiting for the punchline, or possibly, may have lost the thread completely and does not know what to ask you to find his way back.

A good ID will collect and document your information so he doesn't have to go back to you many times. It is up to you to review what you've given the ID to make sure it is in context, accurate and really is what you wanted to include after you see it in the program. The review process makes sure you provided the information you intended to include and that the ID understood it and presented it appropriately.

Tips for Working with Your Instructional Designer

While it is the ID's job – or his manager's job – to assemble questions, propose an interview and review schedule, and ask you to fill in gaps, that process may not always happen flawlessly. Even if it does, it helps for you to be aware that you can make contributions to the successful completion of a training program by keeping a few simple rules in mind.

1. **Organization** - If the steps or flow of the program that the ID has outlined for you do not make sense, put them in a logical sequence. Nobody understands the context of the material better than you and that includes the ID.

2. **Timeliness** – Be available for interviews and do reviews on time.

3. **Scheduling Conflicts** – Anticipate and avoid scheduling conflicts. This seems obvious, but you will find that sometimes your regular work may directly conflict with meeting your SME obligation. If you are in a job where this can occur, plan for this contingency. For example, ask

the ID if you can work ahead on your deadline for your review, comments and sign-offs. The ID, and probably also a graphic designer, computer programmer, project manager and an editor – at the very least – have their work scheduled around your deadline, too. Time is money all the way around. While the time and money associated with the cost of developing the training program may not be obvious to you, other people's deadlines and budgets are affected by your ability to fit this obligation into your schedule. Don't assume yours is the only project the ID is working on and that they have the flexibility to adjust to last-minute scheduling changes.

4. **Accuracy** – Provide the information requested and double-check to make sure it is correct when you get drafts of the program (and yes, you may receive more than one!). This seems simple enough and may even seem insulting to mention, but it wouldn't be here if failure to check information didn't happen.

5. **Sign-Offs** – Sign off at pre-agreed checkpoints, and make sure you have checked the accuracy of the information when you do. If you are working with a contract ID from outside your company, there is probably a contract in place between the training organization and your company that makes your company responsible for content after you affix your signature to it. If you sign off on incorrect information, it will cost your company when the project goes into overruns for corrections or scope creep. Internally, your sign-off means the program is going to

be finalized, packaged and used by learners who are your coworkers. Your sign-off not only is the hallmark of your credibility, but it affects the performance of other people in your organization.

6. **Blind Spots** – We all have them. Frequently, we develop blind spots as a result of our success; failures are more likely to call us up short and require us to be careful and thorough. Because you are the SME, let's assume you've met with a lot of success in your life, and that makes you vulnerable to blind spots. Think through the eyes of a novice when you are explaining details to your ID.

At this point, I am going to excerpt an article from SmartBlogs from SmartBrief[5] by James DeSilva with his permission because it specifically addresses the issue of the shortcomings of experts in a very direct and meaningful way.

DeSilva recalls this story about former British Prime Minister Tony Blair: Blair admitted that it wasn't until he left office that he learned he didn't know what he didn't know. No longer being Prime Minister gave him a new perspective on the world. This eye-opener triggered the following three observations by DeSilva in a blog entitled, "Do You Know How Much You Don't Know?":

- *Admitting surprise at being uninformed is not just for the arrogant. Sure, it seems absurd that Blair only realized in recent years the breadth of what he doesn't*

---

[5] Published on April 22, 2013 at http://smartblogs.com/leadership/2013/04/22/do-you-know-how-much-you-dont-know/. Special thanks to SmartBlogs from SmartBriefs and author James DeSilva for permission to reprint.

understand, but let's think of it on a micro level. How many of us are knowledgeable about our day-to-day business — and also curious and on the watch for threats and trends — yet will be caught off-guard by something that will later seem obvious? Arrogance is only one of many possible factors behind such a failing.

- **Being blind to what we don't know can be a byproduct of success and necessity.** *This is somewhat of a good thing. After all, many of us have advanced by being good at what we do, and by an ability to learn and apply new information. Blair said the toughest problems are difficult because they cannot be avoided. At some point, we must make a decision based on what we know, however incomplete. The danger here is twofold: We begin to regard our knowledge and business intelligence not as incomplete, but as a compendium of everything relevant. This mistaken belief can become reinforced if we then conflate the act of making decisions with being informed. Even successful decisions and an open mind don't remove the risk of blind spots. It's a lot easier to make adjustments in reaction to failure than after success.*

- **Being curious doesn't mean being impulsive.** *Learning more about people, cultures and concepts doesn't mean abrupt changes in mindset, beliefs or strategy. But bringing in different perspectives, combined with reflection and analysis, can help you more accurately calculate what you know and what you don't.*

Top Ten Tips for Providing Great Information

1. Think of the instructional designer (ID) as a court reporter. The ID will take note of everything you say and will later use those notes to create content in the training program.

2. Keep in mind that procedures and knowledge are often being written for new hires, not seasoned experts. Remember that a new hire needs to know every single step in a procedure and needs explanations of complex concepts. For example, pressing the "enter" key after an action might seem like old hat to you, but would a new hire know to do it?

3. In addition to giving the *whats*, remember to give the *whos, whens and whys*. When you're giving instructions for completing a specific action, don't forget to tell the ID *who* the action will affect, *when* the action will take place in relation to the entire process, and *why* the action needs to be completed. Context is critical to understanding.

4. When giving Introductions for individual sections of a learning program, aim for the overall picture approach. Think of the best way to describe the reason for the section to a new hire. Again, look at the *who, when* and *why*, in addition to the *what*.

    Poor Introduction: "The following procedures will allow you to set up a Basic Control Account."

Why is this poor? This sentence only describes *what* the learner is expected to know.

Good Introduction: Before clients can be enrolled in the Corporate Travel program, a Basic Control Account (BCA) needs to be established. BCA is the lowest level of a company's Corporate account hierarchy structure. All clients fall under a BCA. The following are steps for setting up a Basic Control Account. When the BCA is set up, you can enroll individual clients.

Why is this good? The paragraph describes *what* the learner is expected to do, *when* they are expected to do it, *who* is affected and *why* they are performing the task.

5. Remember that the ID only knows what you have told him. Consider yourself the information expert and the ID the novice. Inaccurate procedures arise when an ID attempts to interpret ideas or fill in missing links of information. To avoid misinterpretation, think through the wording of a step in your head first, and then say it aloud to the ID. If you have doubts about your wording, jot it down on paper. Before continuing to the next step, be sure to ask the ID, "Did you get that down?"

6. When giving information to the ID, stay on track. Avoid extraneous information that does not pertain to the specific section you are documenting. Don't be afraid to break procedures into multiple sections to make the training more user-friendly. A good rule is to limit procedure steps

to about 10. A procedure may have 20 steps, but make that the exception, not the rule. If the number of steps becomes excessive, break a process into smaller procedures.

7. While shortcuts are advantageous to someone who has worked in the department for a while, they are usually confusing to a new person. Give *all* the steps to a procedure when you are with an ID. Before giving information to the ID, ask yourself, "Is this our organization's best practice?"

8. If you make a change when reviewing a training document, note your change directly on the page next to the information you are correcting whether using a review function in an electronic document or affixing a sticky note to a hard copy. Be clear about the change. Try to avoid ambiguous statements such as "No! This step needs rework." or "More information needed here." Instead, supply specific information so the ID can easily make the corrections without coming back to you for a second review process. Try to use statements such as, "Add: Move the cursor to the next line before proceeding."

9. Before the end of your session, take the time to review the information you discussed. The goal is to document the procedures and concepts accurately the first time. Feel free to ask the ID to read your information back to you. As you are listening, pretend the procedure is totally new to you and imagine performing the steps or using the information as the ID repeats it.

10. Whenever possible, provide the ID with hard copy documentation. For example, if you are working with software, provide screen prints both blank and completed for reference with visible drop-down menus. If you are referencing an article you have written, provide the article. If you have a slide presentation that you have delivered on the topic, provide that. You may have charts, graphics and sources in those materials that can be used in the training program.

CHAPTER 6.

Project Leadership: Managing the Training Program Process

Advice for Project Managers, Senior Directors and Department Leaders

Good processes cannot compensate for lack of competence; however, competence is not sufficient without good processes.

Whether you are in charge of a training department, managing an instructional design group or overseeing the people involved in creating training, you have some ability to influence the flow of content collection and review.

You may be managing timelines and resources for billing and tracking progress on a training program, or you may be intimately involved in the training program development as an instructional design manager. Below are a few guidelines that can help you keep track of your instructional designer and their subject matter expert to make sure they are getting what they need, on time and intact.

The Value of Processes

When a process is in place, everyone understands *what* needs to happen, *when* it needs to happen, and *how* it needs to happen.

Virtually every successful project has benefitted from a plan and good processes. Conversely, projects that lack a plan and good processes face obstacles. Without established processes, people working on a training project are just "making it up as they go along." That is a prescription for cost overruns, missed deadlines and poor work products. Lack of good processes also lays the foundation for many misunderstandings among people who are working together.

Processes need to be in place at the beginning of the project, before the first meeting, so everyone on a project enters it with clear direction. To avoid a project that can careen out of control, institute processes before the work begins. Establish controls and clear roles at the start to set expectations and patterns for success.

When processes are instituted partway through a project, everyone knows that there was not a plan at the outset, and at the very least, people lose respect for the project. If you start a project without established processes, competent people who are involved will make sure that it is concluded successfully. However, if a project careens out of control and a "leader" emerges late in the game with new processes to try to wrangle a project into her control, its failure is nearly guaranteed. You will have casualties among competent people, and the project itself will become a casualty, as well.

Lead, Follow or Get Out of the Way

Leaders need to be present and good processes in place at the outset. It is easy to follow a plan that everyone understands; it is impossible to follow a plan that is haphazard, ill-conceived or put in place after work has begun. It makes good sense to understand and establish good processes for training designers and their SMEs as part of your training development program. Chapter 7 will give you best practice materials that will assist you in managing their work.

In the event that a leader, manager, director or designer leaves in the middle of a project, established best practices and recognized controls will allow the project to continue on course with minimal disruption. A wise leader, manager or director entering a well-managed project midstream will learn the processes and assume command of the ongoing plan for continuity. One of the basic tenets of good leadership is to do nothing for the first six months after you take over an organization. That rule extends to managing a project that is underway; it is best practice to observe and appraise the situation before making major changes. A competent leader coming into a well-managed project will allow it to proceed on course without disruption. A competent leader coming into a poorly managed project can either allow it to careen to its conclusion or end it and start again later.

In the event there is a change in leadership and no processes in place, you are nearly guaranteed to have mayhem. The best course of action is to end the effort and begin again with new people, established processes and re-defined goals.

Setting the Stage for Success – The Project Charter

You can set the stage for success by being clear up front about expectations. To start, make sure you have written a comprehensive Project Charter that requires stakeholders to sign and acknowledge the resources needed to complete the training program successfully. A sample Project Charter is included in Chapter 7 Tools for *Working with SMEs*. The Project Charter will define the parameters of the project, the essential personnel, and the lines of responsibility. It should address your needs for the appropriate personnel, including SMEs, from the client side.

Proactive SME Management

A detailed Project Charter that includes sign-off from all major stakeholders can give you some clout when outlining the terms of engagement with your SME. You can build in failsafe mechanisms for a SME that consistently misses or is late for appointments. Depending on the resources in the corporation, you may or may not be able to actually hold your SME accountable, but having such clauses at least sets expectations at the beginning of the relationship and gives you a ripcord if you need one.

When you begin a relationship with a SME, make sure they understand that being a SME is a very important job. Their work as a training asset helps raise the performance and outcomes of the entire organization. Subject matter experts who share their knowledge ensure new people to the company or department can learn their jobs and be valuable employees. Companies are only as good as their employees. That's why companies invest in people by providing instructionally-sound training that equips them with the skills and knowledge they need to do their jobs.

By making sure SMEs understand their importance and the relevance of good training to the health of the organization, you are helping the company achieve their performance objectives. And by detailing the SME's involvement at the outset and holding them accountable, the instructional designer and project manager are offering a valuable service, as well.

Pitfalls of Delegating

Another basic tenet of leadership is that *responsibility, accountability* and *authority* are intertwined. If a person has only one or two of these without all three, problems are guaranteed.

If you are the leader, manager or director of a training project, and you have the ultimate responsibility for its success, you need to delegate clearly and wisely any of the responsibility, accountability and authority that belongs to you.

For example, if you have a new ID who is not familiar with your company, or you are using a contract ID, it is important to hold regular meetings with the customer and provide updates to the customer on the status of the project. Delegate, don't abdicate.

If you choose to have a new ID take charge of a project or train her to take over projects in the future, make sure she is working closely with an experienced senior person every step of the way. The senior person's signature must be attached to everything needing approval.

Do not ask a contract ID to perform the work of a leader in your organization. Period. An outside contractor should *never* have the authority to schedule the time of your other staff, be it your SME or a graphic designer. And the contract ID's signature should not appear on updates or memos to staff without a signoff from you. A contract ID is external to your organization and does not have the same level of responsibility or accountability to your client as a full-time employee. *Note:* This applies strictly to contract IDs. This stricture obviously does not apply to contract CEOs, COOs, PMs etc., as it is their role to take control of the organization or project.

Common Sense Guidelines

Good leadership and project management principles will help you manage the process of content collection between an ID and their SME. Here are a few common sense – but important – guidelines to managing your training designers who are *Working with SMEs*:

- Define the human resources. Make sure you have assigned the correct SMEs and training designers to the project.

- Have a toolkit of templates for collecting, organizing and reviewing content. Make sure your ID and your SME have them, understand them and use them, although expect they may modify them to meet the needs of the project at hand.

- Schedule milestones or make sure they are in place. If you aren't the project manager, stay in contact with the PM at regular intervals.

- Check in with the ID to make sure she is getting what she needs from her SME.

- If there appears to be content or deadline problems, check in with the SME to make sure she is able to provide what is needed, can stay on schedule, and is comfortable with the work product being created by the ID.

- Schedule regular updates from the PM outlining progress to everyone involved in the process; weekly updates are recommended.

- Make sure everyone is clear about their level of responsibility and authority.

CHAPTER 7.

Tools for Managing an ID Project

When a process is in place, everyone understands what needs to happen, when it needs to happen, and how it needs to happen.

A few basic documents and procedures can make *Working with SME's* a smooth process. In this chapter, we offer some templates that you can use or modify to fit the needs of your project or organization.

- Project Charter
- Scope of Project
- Subject Matter Expert Contact List
- Content Gathering Session Cover Sheet
- Process Map Sample
- SME Review Log
- Acknowledgment of Review
- After Action Review Form

Project Charter

Purpose of the Charter
The project charter defines the scope, objectives and overall approach for the work to be completed. It is a critical element for initiating, planning, executing, controlling, and assessing the project. It is an initial single point of reference on the project for project goals and objectives, scope, estimates, roles and responsibilities and timelines. In addition, it serves as a contract between the Project Team and the Project Sponsors, stating what will be delivered according to the agreed upon budget, time constraints, risks, resources, and standards.

About The Client
[Describes the client's business and mission.]

Project Overview
[Describes the topic(s) to be trained and the audiences who are the targets of the training.]

Project Goals
[Describes the goals of the project and how they tie to the client's business objectives.]

Expected Outcomes
[Lists the desired outcomes of the training, including what employees will be able to do and the effect they will have on performance and business outcomes.]

Content
[Describes the topics and length of full curriculum to be developed.]

Audience
[Lists who will be trained.]

Instructor-led training (ILT)/eLearning requirements:
[Lists the software and components of training to be developed (i.e., Articulate, PowerPoint, Facilitator's Guide, Mentoring Guide, Job Aides, Posters, Marketing Materials, etc.]

Assessment and Evaluation:
[Describes what type of assessments will be included in the training, how trainee competency will be evaluated and acknowledged and how the training program will be evaluated.]

Upfront Planning, Ongoing Project Management and Project Schedule
[Create a project plan using a program such as MS Project, Smartsheet, Unfuddle, Excel or create one of your own like the sample provided. A detailed project plan will include milestones for information gathering, review cycles and signoffs. It may include provisions for alpha, beta and final versions.]

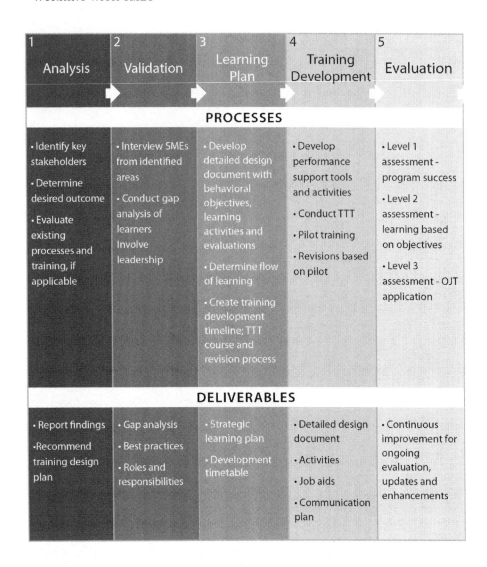

1 Analysis	2 Validation	3 Learning Plan	4 Training Development	5 Evaluation
PROCESSES				
• Identify key stakeholders • Determine desired outcome • Evaluate existing processes and training, if applicable	• Interview SMEs from identified areas • Conduct gap analysis of learners Involve leadership	• Develop detailed design document with behavioral objectives, learning activities and evaluations • Determine flow of learning • Create training development timeline; TTT course and revision process	• Develop performance support tools and activities • Conduct TTT • Pilot training • Revisions based on pilot	• Level 1 assessment - program success • Level 2 assessment - learning based on objectives • Level 3 assessment - OJT application
DELIVERABLES				
• Report findings •Recommend training design plan	• Gap analysis • Best practices • Roles and responsibilities	• Strategic learning plan • Development timetable	• Detailed design document • Activities • Job aids • Communication plan	• Continuous improvement for ongoing evaluation, updates and enhancements

Assumptions

[Describes any specific, unusual or mandatory requirements to be considered in the design, development, delivery and evaluation of the training program.]

Project Alerts

Project alerts will be documented in the project plan. Issues that require immediate attention should be addressed with the Project Manager and Project Sponsor. The guidelines for priority criteria should be used to determine issue priority.

Priority Criteria
1. High-priority/critical-path issue; requires immediate follow-up and resolution.
2. Medium-priority issue; requires follow-up before completion of next project milestone.
3. Low-priority issue; to be resolved prior to project completion.
4. Closed issue.

Project Style Guidelines
[Describes branding of materials, style guidelines for written and graphic content, etc.]

Roles and Responsibilities

Project Team Members	
Role	Person
Executive Sponsor/Owner	
Senior Consultant/Project Manager	
Senior Consultant	
Editor/QA	
Client Relationship Manager	
Design Team	
Instructional Designer	
Graphic Designer	
Client Project Manager	
Client Stakeholders/Customers	

Scope of Project

The scope of the project requires best-guess estimates by project owners to be determined in cooperation with managers, instructional designers (IDs), subject matter experts (SMEs) and other stakeholders to establish deadline, milestone and budget parameters. The answers to these questions will provide the basis of any contractual relationships.

Scope of Project
Title of Program:
Length of Program:
Development Hours/Training Hours*:
Training for Subject/Department:
Training Project Manager:
Subject/Department Project Owner:
Delivery Platform:
Delivery Platform:
Delivery/Launch Date:
Project budget in FTEs/dollars:
Instructional Designer(s) Assigned:
Subject Matter Expert(s) Assigned:
Other Stakeholders/Sign-off Authority:
Other Stakeholders/Sign-off Authority:
Other Stakeholders/Sign-off Authority:

*Depending on the delivery platform and other factors regarding the personnel and subject matter involved, the average number of development hours per delivery training time will vary widely. Standard development time for instructor-led training is 40:1; elearning ratios can be much higher. Your estimates will be just that – estimates – based on your prior experience developing similar training. Add time to your best-guess estimate to account for unknowns and identified risks, such as new IDs and new subject matter.

Subject Matter Expert Contact List

Subject Matter Expert Contact List				
Job Number:				
Job Title:				
Company:				
Client (who's paying)/Title:				
Client Phone, Fax and Email:				
Contract Start Date:				
Description of Work:				
Lead Developer:				
Contact/SME Name	Department/ Title/Topic	Phone Number	Email	Availability (best time, days, weeks)

Content Gathering Cover Sheet

Ideally, content gathering sessions are no longer than two hours. This cover sheet ensures that the meeting and its contents are documented and approved. In most complicated programs, more than one session is needed. The key to a successful interview is to read any preparatory materials provided by the SME. If no preparatory materials are provided, the ID should do some research on the topic to prepare good questions.

Content Gathering Session Cover Sheet

Training Program Name:
Instructional Designer:
Subject Matter Expert:
Date/time of Interview:
Oral interview (note time/length/recording):
Interview transcription checked by ID, approved by SME:
List of prepared questions attached:
Receipt of Information:
Materials (list ppts, reports, web links, etc.):
o Provided before interview:
o Provided during interview:
o To be provided after the interview:
Physical file and/or electronic file for Client Assets (i.e., all materials provided to create the training program):

Note: The importance of starting with a list of prepared questions cannot be over-emphasized. A sample of prepared questions is provided in Chapter 8. As a rule, a prepared question list should start with establishing some very basic information such as spelling the name and title of the SME correctly, noting the time and date of the interview, and asking a few broad questions to begin. Those questions will have several branches of progressive detail. Leave time for questions in response to answers. In general, a great interview is flexible enough to pursue the unexpected, very important pieces of information gleaned through the interview process. In training particularly, the interviewer and interviewee will continue to check their questions and answers against the pre-determined learning objectives for the course during the interview to be sure they are staying on track.

Documentation Map

Purpose of this document: Training, documentation and process specialists use this process to capture steps involved in performing a task. Process maps provide a guide for more detailed step-by-step procedures for instructional design.

Task Name:

System or screen [if software]:

Role: [who performs task]

DIFT* Rating: D__ I__ F__ T__

Difficulty - Task can be reliably performed

1. After employees hear or read about it

2. After employees practice it once

3. After employees practice at least 1 to 4 times

4. While using a job aid after training

5. With help from co-worker after training

Importance/Consequence of Error

1. No consequence to customer

2. Minimal negative impact to customer

3. Major impact on customer

4. Violation of company policy

5. Violation of state/federal law(s)

Ask SME for 3 to 5 sentence summary of the task

↓

Determine if process is complex with multiple segments. If so, tile the processes to create a pathway for each segment

↓

Complete initial summary of who, what, why with roles identified

↓

Capture sequential steps & decisions SME uses to perform the task

↓

Recap steps in process map and check with SME for accuracy and clarity

↓

Frequency

1. Hourly

2. Daily

3. Weekly

4. Monthly

5. Quarterly

6. Annually

Time in increments

1. Minutes

2. Hours

3. Days

Recap summary and additional information to support process and give context

Determine DIFT rating

Create process map in a replicable job aid and file in a repository (eg. LMS, software documentation)

*Note on the DIFT rating: The rating is important to determine the level of difficulty of the task to ensure it is role-appropriate, time to mastery and importance of repetition for performance support.

SME Review Log

This is a sample spreadsheet that is helpful in collecting comments from multiple reviewers. If only one reviewer is making changes, it is possible to track them in the draft document itself using Track Changes in Word, the Comment function in slide presentation software and word processing software or the Review function in an eLearning program. However, when more than one person reviews a program, which is typically the case in most programs, it is helpful to use a spreadsheet to collect all the comments. After the comments are collected, one person – either an editor or the ID – can make all the changes into the final document for consistency.

Note in this sample review log that there are two review log pages – one for a review of version 1 of the training program and one for changes after the pilot program has been presented. When following ADDIE, the pilot program provides the opportunity for Evaluation using at least Kirkpatrick's first and second level evaluations. The evaluations provide the opportunity to make revisions to polish the program.

Training Program Review Log – Spreadsheet Format

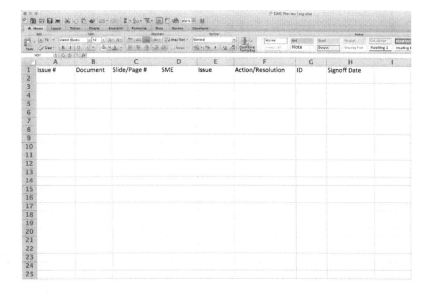

Acknowledgment of Review

Training Program Title:
Subject Matter Expert(s):
Team Leader/ Manager:
Instructional Designer:

I understand that the accuracy of the attached document is the responsibility of client/department employees. By signing below, I am verifying that I have thoroughly read the document for content, detail and accuracy. To the best of my knowledge, the document is correct, except where notated.

NOTE: Expected turnaround time is three (3) business days. It is the responsibility of the Team Leader to compile comments into a single document and submit to the training designer.

1	Date Received:	I approve the FINAL draft of the *DESIGN SPECS* with changes noted.	Subject Matter Expert's Signature:
2	Date Received:	I approve the FINAL draft of the *DESIGN SPECS* with changes noted.	Team Leader/Manager's Signature:
3	Date Received:	I approve the FIRST draft of the *TRAINING MATERIALS* with changes noted.	Subject Matter Expert's Signature:
4	Date Received:	I approve the FINAL draft of the *TRAINING MATERIALS* with changes noted.	Team Leader/Manager's Signature:
5	Date Received:	I approve the FINAL draft of the *TRAINING MATERIALS* as is (ready to print or upload).	Director/Client's Signature:

Proofing Tips:

✓ Do the behavioral objectives cover what employees should be able to do after the training?

✓ Does the content cover the behavioral objectives?

✓ Would a new employee, or the employee at the level to which the materials are aimed, be able to follow and understand the training?

✓ Are all the steps and supporting information for the processes or topic covered?

✓ Have you checked all client specific information, terms, forms, systems, processes or report names for accuracy?

✓ Could any part of the materials use further explanation to increase clarity beyond that which is covered?

✓ Do your corrections precisely indicate what changes are needed, leaving no room for misinterpretation by training and instructional designers or other company employees?

Review and Sign-off Sheet

Training Program:

I understand that the accuracy of the attached documents is the responsibility of client's/department's employees. By signing below, I am verifying that I have thoroughly read the document for content, detail and accuracy. To the best of my knowledge, the document is correct, except where noted.

NOTE: If more than one set of comments exists for a single document, it is the responsibility of the client's/department's project manager to compile comments and submit one copy to the training department.

#	Document Title	1st Draft Approval SME		Final Approval SME		Final Approval TEAM LEADER		Final Approval DIRECTOR
		Initials	Date	Initials	Date	Initials	Date	Initials
1								
2								
3								
4								
5								
6								

After-Action Review

Any program or project deserves an After-Action Review. This is just as true in corporate training as it is in military campaigns. Sometimes known as "the post-mortem" or "lessons learned", the practice of retrospectively reviewing the actions and results of a project is an essential part of winding down, getting resolution, learning and moving on.

Training Program Project Name:

Project Team:

A successful After-Action Review will:

✓ Focus directly on the intended goals, tasks and outcomes.
✓ Attempt to discover what actually happened and why.
✓ Encourage participants to discuss important lessons learned.
✓ Capture process improvements for future projects.
✓ Applaud the team's successes.

An After-Action Review does not:

✓ Judge success or failure.
✓ Assign blame to anyone.

What were our intended results?	What were our actual results?	What caused our results?

What worked well that we will do again next time?

What will we do differently next time?

CHAPTER 8.

Sample Training Program Process Documents in Action

Keeping It Simple

I am a big proponent of getting things done. Sometimes our obsession with *how* to get things done gets in the way of actually getting them done. In trying to avoid that pitfall, I boiled down my experiences with projects that have gone swimmingly and those that have been long, convoluted exercises in futility to come up with a plan for simplicity.

This is not to deny the fact that you can have very complex training programs with many modules, many audiences, and a long rollout period that require great planning and managing a lot of moving parts. Simplicity, in those cases, would hurt success.

You will need a matrix of the components to manage the project to keep it under control.

However, about half the programs I've encountered can benefit from the following approach. It is offered in the spirit that readers will call on their own experiences and knowledge of how they work best, and adjust this recommendation to their own situations.

With that in mind, I offer a few thoughts on ways to keep development simple and efficient:

- Find people who perform well and let them do their jobs.

- Keep the number of people limited to the number necessary to get the good result.

- Good processes are a guide and need to allow for flexibility.

- Fewer steps are better. These seven steps should allow for a single, simple module of 30 minutes of live slide presentation-based training to two hours of eLearning content go from concept to delivery in three to six weeks.

Table 8.1: Simple Project Flow in Seven Steps

Step	Who	Estimated Time
1. Kickoff a project and define it*	Stakeholders	1 day
2. Create an outline that includes a beginning, goal and milestones	Project lead/ID	2 days
3. Fill in outline with detail – work with SME's	ID/SME/PM with input from stakeholders	1 week to 1 month
4. Edit/refine	Editor/ID	2 days: 1 day for overview, 1 day for editing
5. Approve	All stakeholder signoffs and last minute revisions	3 days
6. Final tweaks	ID	1 day
7. Signoff	All stakeholders indicate final approval	1 day
Implement and Evaluate!	Deliver final program	

*Assumes discussions have already determined the type of training program and its goal in advance of actually putting the project and its scope to paper. See the Project Charter and Scope of Project documents in Chapter 7.

Sample Training Program: Stellar Customer Service in SMEville

Somewhere in a fictional world, there is a Merry Band of IDs who live in the land of SMEville. They are developing yet another training program to keep their already cheerful residents happy. SMEville prides itself on customer service. From the barber shop to the gas station, every business greets its customer with a smile.

This doesn't happen by accident. Great training is the bedrock of SMEville's reputation for customer service. Travelers along Route E-I-E-I-O love to stop at this small town, take in the sights of its quaint village square and smell its bakeries at dawn. Most of all, visitors enjoy the friendly townsfolk.

In order to keep order, the Village Wise Ones long ago instituted publicly-sponsored customer service training programs that any business in town is able to access – for free! The Village Wise Ones believe it is a prudent use of tax dollars to keep the town's services flowing smoothly, support everyone in their quest to be happy, and thus encourage the onslaught of visitors that fill SMEville's coffers with out-of-town coins.

The Village Wise Ones asked the Merry Band of IDs to update the town's customer service training program. So they have. Jill Askit was assigned the position of instructional designer for this all-important program, and Jack Knowit is the SME assigned to the project.

And since the Merry Band of IDs do everything properly, they have documented their procedures and generously agreed to allow us to print them here, in our book, on *Working with SMEs*. After all, it's in the town's charter that everyone be cheerful and helpful at all times.

By reading all the documentation provided by SMEville, you will be able to learn how the project was developed and executed.

Customer Service in SMEville: How to Develop Warm Customer Relations

Scope of Project	
Title of Program	Warm Customer Relations
Length of Program	1.0 hour
Delivery Platform	Instructor-Led Training
Delivery/Launch Date	January 1
Development Hours/Training Hour	40:1
Training for Subject/Department	Personnel
Training Project Manager	
Other Stakeholders/Sign-Off Authority	
Subject/Department Project Owner	
Instructional Designer(s) Assigned	
Subject Matter Expert(s) Assigned	
Project Budget in FTEs/Dollars	

Subject Matter Expert Contact List

Job Number:	2014-001
Job Title:	Warm Customer Service
Company:	SMEville
Client (who's paying)/Title:	SMEville Municipal Human Resource Department
Client Phone, Fax and Email:	Ph: 555-555-1212 email: sally.smiles@smeeville.gov
Contract Start Date:	11/1/2013
Description of Work:	Develop a one-hour instructor led training program with PowerPoint slides, participant handouts and a facilitator guide.
Lead Developer:	Jill Askit

Contact/SME Name	Department/ Title/Topic	Phone Number	Email	Availability
Jack Knowit	Consultant	555.555.1313	Jack.Knowit@me.com	M, W, Th 9-12
Sally Smiles	SMEville HR	555.555.1212	Sally.Smiles@me.com	M-F 9-5

Content Gathering Session Cover Sheet

Content Gathering Session Cover Sheet

Training Program Name:
Instructional Designer:
Subject Matter Expert:
Date/time of Interview:
Oral interview (note time/length/recording):
Interview transcription checked by ID, approved by SME:
List of prepared questions attached:
Receipt of Information:
Materials (list ppts, reports, web links, etc.):
o Provided before interview:
o Provided during interview:
o To be provided after the interview:
Physical file and/or electronic file for Client Assets (i.e., all materials provided to create the training program):

Jill's Prepared Interview Questions

Here are the questions that Jill prepared in advance for her first general interview with Jack, the SME. After reviewing the current training and some of the new information, she will need to update the program. She assumes that after she has conducted this interview and written a first rough draft, she will have more questions and need more details to refine the program. She schedules a second interview with Jack a few days later so they can have the first draft in front of them as she gathers more detail. The results of this interview and her first draft will dictate the content of the second interview.

Note to self: Check spelling of name, his organization, his title.

1. According to the latest study by your organization, you found that when you approach a situation with a positive attitude, you are likely to get a better result. Why does that happen?

2. How does this differ from what we are currently teaching our employees about customer service?

3. What changes can our employees make to provide better customer service based on your latest data? Specifically, can you give me some simple steps that people can remember to help them perform their jobs better?

4. Can you provide me with the details of the studies (some charts and graphs that I can use in the slide presentation)?

5. What are some exercises that we can do at the live training session to teach and reinforce these new skills and best practices? Specifically, let's record the activity step-by-step so I can recreate it accurately in the training materials.

Note to self: Confirm when and how you will receive the charts and graphs you have requested. Confirm date, time and place of next interview.

SME Review Log

This is the spreadsheet that Jack Knowit and Sally Smiles used to assemble their remarks and revisions for the Warm Customer Relations training module.

Sample Review Log for Warm Customer Relation

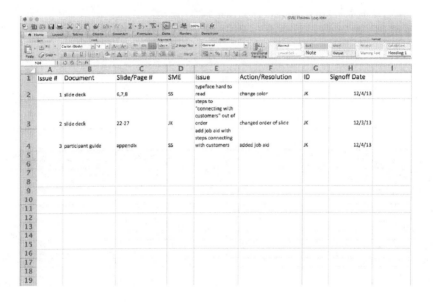

	A	B	C	D	E	F	G	H	I
1	Issue #	Document	Slide/Page #	SME	Issue	Action/Resolution	ID	Signoff Date	
2	1	slide deck	6,7,8	SS	typeface hard to read	change color	JK	12/4/13	
3	2	slide deck	22-27	JK	steps to "connecting with customers" out of order	changed order of slide	JK	12/3/13	
4	3	participant guide	appendix	SS	add job aid with steps connecting with customers	added job aid	JK	12/4/13	
5									
6									
7									
8									
9									
10									
11									
12									
13									
14									
15									
16									
17									
18									
19									

Acknowledgment of Review

Training Program Title: Warm Customer Relations
Subject Matter Expert(s): Jack Knowit and Sally Smiles
Team Leader/ Manager: Jane Perfect
Instructional Designer: Jill Askit

I understand that the accuracy of the attached document is the responsibility of client/department employees. By signing below, I am verifying that I have thoroughly read the document for content, detail and accuracy. To the best of my knowledge, the document is correct, except where noted.

NOTE: Expected turnaround time is three (3) business days. If more than one set of comments exists for a single document, it is the responsibility of the Team Leader to compile comments and submit one copy to the training designer.

1	Date Received: 11/1/2013	I approve the FINAL draft of the *DESIGN SPECS* with changes noted.	Subject Matter Expert's Signature: Jack Knowit, Sally Smiles
2	Date Received: 11/1/2013	I approve the FINAL draft of the *DESIGN SPECS* with changes noted.	Team Leader/Manager's Signature: Jane Perfect
3	Date Received: 12/1/2013	I approve the FIRST draft of the *TRAINING MATERIALS* with changes noted.	Subject Matter Expert's Signature: Jack Knowit, Sally Smiles
4	Date Received: 12/7/2013	I approve the FINAL draft of the *TRAINING MATERIALS* with changes noted.	Team Leader/Manager's Signature: Jane Perfect
5	Date Received: 12/15/2013	I approve the FINAL draft of the *TRAINING MATERIALS* as is (ready to print or upload).	Director/Client's Signature: John Goodman

Proofing Tips:

✓ Do the behavioral objectives cover what employees should be able to do after the training?

✓ Does the content cover the behavioral objectives?

✓ Would a new employee, or the employee at the level to which the materials are aimed, be able to follow and understand the training?

✓ Are all the steps and supporting information for the processes or topic covered?

✓ Have you checked all client specific information, terms, forms, systems, processes or report names for accuracy?

✓ Could any part of the materials use further explanation to increase clarity beyond that which is covered?

✓ Do your corrections precisely indicate what changes are needed, leaving no room for misinterpretation by training and instructional designers or other company employees?

After-Action Review

Training Program Project Name: Warm Customer Relations
Project Team: Jane Perfect, Sally Smiles, Jill Askit, Jack Knowit, John Goodman

What were our intended results?	What were our actual results?	What caused our results?
Improve customer relations by teaching our employees good rapport skills	Visitor complaints down from 1 in Q3 2013 to 0 in Q2 2014	May have been the training, but cannot be absolutely certain. Other factors, such as more free ice cream at the Visitors' Center, may have influenced positive visitor experience.
Increase number of visitors to the Visitors' Center	Visitors increased by 10% from Q2 2013 to Q2 2014	May be the training, but cannot be certain. May be attributed to the new Visitors' Center billboard on the interstate.
Increase revenue from tourism at the Visitors' Center	Revenue flat from Q2 2013 to Q2 2014	May have been the free ice cream that suppressed the demand for snacks and affected revenue at the soda shoppe despite increase in visitors.

What worked well that we will do again next time?
Employees enjoyed the training session, especially Jack Knowit's new exercises on warm human interactions. Everyone felt good at the end of the session. We will repeat this exercise when we train the next group of employees.
The participant handouts were well-received and the employees are using the job aids at their work stations. We will keep the job aids in the next participant guide.

What will we do differently next time?

We underestimated the amount of time we would spend on the exercise, and the training ran over by 15 minutes. We will cut down the number of informational slides with charts and graphs, and keep the exercise intact.

We will change the font color on slides 6, 7, and 8 to black. They were hard to read against the background.

Performance Support in SMEville

The Warm Customer Relations training program was well received both by the employees and the trainers involved in the sessions. The human resource manager was pleased and asked that the program be expanded for the following year to include a module on Handling Difficult Customers.

Evaluating the success of a program can be as simple as using a smile sheet to find out if the attendees enjoyed the session or by developing an assessment that directly measures the learner's comprehension. In the case of SMEville's warm customer relations training, success could also be gauged by the number of visitors to SMEville and revenue from tourists.

As trainers, we also measure success when our clients return to us to develop more training for them.

In SMEville, Jill Askit will be busy next year working with Jack Knowit again as they explore ways to overcome challenges with customers. The true measure of success is their ongoing relationship with each other and with the good folks at SMEville municipal services.

EPILOGUE

I want to express my sincere gratitude and appreciation to you, the readers, for taking the time to spend with this book. I value you as colleagues in the continuous search for improvement. I believe that success is built on great people supported by good processes. In this book, I am sharing some processes that have worked for me, my clients and supported with tools from Jonena Relth's TBD Consulting.

It is important to emphasize, at this point, that each situation is different. The advice for *Working with SMEs* takes into consideration many situations and builds in flexibility for the variability of your experiences. In the chapter on SMEville, I deliberately simplified the process to make it accessible and brief. Please adapt the tips and tools for each training program to allow for success with your unique trainers, learners, subject matter and organizations.

Most of all, I look forward to hearing from you as colleagues and clients as I continue to refine the art of Working with SMEs in the spirit of continuous process improvement.

You are invited to reproduce the tips and tools that are offered in this book with credit to *Working with SMEs: A Guide to Gathering and Organizing Content from Subject Matter Experts.*

Visit:

www.WorkingwithSMEs.com

Cheers,

Peggy Salvatore

ABOUT THE AUTHOR

Peggy Salvatore, MBA

Peggy Salvatore has written many training programs in healthcare as well as on general business topics. Her background includes extensive research, analysis and writing for professional journal articles, white papers and executive background briefings on a broad range of health policy issues. She was a political reporter and columnist and covered the 1988 Republican National Convention before leaving daily journalism for business. She holds an MBA with a concentration in strategy and economics. Peggy is the mother of three wonderfully grown children and lives midway between Philadelphia and New York City.

NOTES

_____

_____

_____

_____

_____

_____

_____

_____

_____

_____